The Great White SHARK

The Great White SHARK

By Jim Crockett

Foreword by Hugh Downs

Copyright ©1989 by Jim Crockett/NLP Inc.
All rights reserved.

Published in 1989 by Arch Cape Press,
a division of dilithium Press, Inc., distributed by
Crown Publishers, Inc., 225 Park Avenue South,
New York, New York 10003.

Printed and Bound in Hong Kong.

Library of Congress Cataloging-in-Publication Data
Crockett, Jim.
The great white shark/Jim Crockett.
p. cm.
Includes index.
ISBN 0-517-66478-X
1. White shark. I. Title
QL638.95.L3C76 1988
597' .31--dc19 87-37345

h g f e d c b a

Graphic design: Wales Christian Ledgerwood, Jim Crockett.
Graphic production: Wales Christian Ledgerwood.

This book is generously dedicated to

. . . my wife, Roberta, who has shared so many dives with me and who has lent me so much encouragement in this book and all that led to it

. . . my children—Cheńoa, Laurenne, Cordell, Kessel, and my stepson Devon—all of whom share my love of nature and my search for truth in whatever we do

. . . and to Rodney, Carl and all the others who have devoted so much of their lives to the study and the experience of the Great White.

Photos & Illustrations

Foreword

THE DEEP HUMAN FASCINATION with sharks may be rooted in something more than fear. There is a theory advanced in the book *Our Face From Fish To Man* by William King Gregory, that the human species is descended from the Devonian shark, one verticil of which evolved into a creature resembling the Australian lungfish, and became a true amphibian, and at the dawn of the Mesozoic Age became a small reptile, which, with the coming of the age of mammals turned into a lemur-like creature, the forerunner of a type of monkey, which in turn grew into a tree-dwelling ape, which came down onto the savannahs of Africa to adopt an upright stance and become the ancestor of modern man.

If this is true, then we're dealing with a relative when we seek out the Great White—a relative far more fearsome than any of the great apes with which we may have common ancestry.

I went into a shark cage a quarter-century ago. This cage had been welded together by diver Elgin Ciampi, and in rough seas it tended to bang you on the head unless you hooked a foot under the lower bars, and then you had the feeling that with an ocean full of sharks you might wind up walking on the stump of an ankle. So you went back to banging your head on the top bars—which of course felt so good when you stopped!

The opportunity, however, to see and photograph, at extremely close range, the most ferocious animal of the sea made it worth the trip. (I believe cage design has improved in a quarter-century.)

To read Jim Crockett's day-by-day account of one of the greatest adventures a human can have, is to live so close to the real thing that it is hardly vicarious. As you read it, I recommend you have a comb handy unless you want people to see you with your hair standing straight up!

— Hugh Downs

CHAPTER ONE

Perspective

FRIEND OF MINE SWEARS he's seen God. I've seen the Great White Shark. We're about even.

There are hundreds of sharks in the sea, but it's the Great White that is the most dangerous, that is the largest of the predatory ones, that is the one taking the biggest bites of whatever it wants to. It swims the oceans almost at will, afraid of nothing. Granted it isn't the only shark credited with attacking humans, but it's the one we fear the most. The Great White Shark has evolved over hundreds of millions of years, and its physiology has adapted perfectly to its environment and metabolism: It can approach much faster animals unnoticed, it can exist in almost any water temperature, it can eat nearly anything, it can survive massive injury, its young can fend for themselves from birth. This is, as we'll see, *the ultimate shark*.

The White Shark has captivated imaginations for endless generations. After all, it preceded humans by 400 million years. There's something mysterious about this captivation, however, since there are only a handful of people who have seen the Great White in open ocean. Even today, there are barely a hundred—including scientists, film crews, authors and tourist-divers—who have intentionally gone in the water with the Great White (and virtually always in steel cages). It's safe to estimate that not more than a thousand people in the world have ever seen a live White in nature, whether in a tangled fish net, on a hefty line, or having been caught by surprise while swimming.

So, why all the worldwide fear? There are more than 350 species of sharks in the oceans—some as short as a foot, others sixty feet long—but mention "shark" to anyone, and they'll imagine something very close to the Great White—huge, torpedo-shaped, and with row after row of knife-like teeth.

There's simply a basic fear we all have when it comes to envisioning the worst possible death. Every culture, every period, has that same horror of being eaten alive. What could possibly be worse? Sure, lions have a history, but when you consider happening upon a lion in the jungle, you also think about jumping out of the way of the charge, about being armed with a rifle—in short, about having a chance. In the water, with a Great White Shark heading for you? It's all over, and you know it. You can't escape; you can't survive. Oh sure, there are a handful of people alive today with White scars. A handful perhaps.

* * * * *

Shark tanks in any aquarium attract the largest crowds. We stare in silence, usually, as the four-foot black-tips glide in their peaceful arcs. Invariably someone is overheard telling a friend a few "facts." And, correct or not, these facts will include something about teeth, something about death.

Only one Great White has lived in captivity. In 1980, nearly 50,000 people packed San Francisco's Steinhart Aquarium for the four days "Sandy" was contained. The three-hundred-pound seven-footer nearly died that week because of disorientation caused by a tiny electrical leak in the tank, and was mercifully released at sea.

Some Whites have been inadvertently caught in fish nets and hauled out of the water, usually to be immediately killed and brought ashore as trophies. Many have been hooked by shark fishermen. But seeing a White on the end of a line, tangled in a net, or trapped in a tank is not seeing the shark in its natural environment. Certainly it may be said that sharks attacking metal cages or ripping apart horsemeat that hangs from a rope isn't seeing them in the wild, either, but it's as close as any of us ought to get. Being in the open water, unprotected, with a Great White, is pure and simple insanity.

Sharks aren't random killers, dripping blood from the corners of their mouths. White Sharks kill for the same reason humans do—to eat. Humans, however, also kill for sport. Sharks don't. If you're in the water with a White, and that White is full from a recent meal, you're in no danger at all. If they've eaten heavily, they can go weeks without food. A satiated Great White won't do any more than circle slowly around, perhaps out of curiosity, and slip silently away. You just never know if they're contented or not. Researchers, time and again, have spent days attracting sharks with meat, fish and blood, only to see their star attractions, now full of bait, leave the area indefinitely while other twenty-pound morsels hang

CHAPTER TWO

In The Cage

YOU'RE ONE OF PERHAPS only a dozen amateur divers ever to go in the underwater cage in search of the Great White Shark of Australia. In each of the prior seven trips that the See and Sea dive travel operators have put together, just five or six people attended, and most of them were authors, professional photographers, filmmakers or researchers. You're a bit apprehensive, but then, so are the rest. Leader Carl Roessler, the brilliant underwater photographer and head of See and Sea Travel, sends divers on hundreds of trips all over the world each year. He can't accompany them all, but the Shark Safari is one he has yet to pass up. With you are a diver/photographer from England with his first book contract for a study of the world's sharks; a French author and cameraman who is on his third book about underwater life; an adventure-seeking doctor who has been on numerous Roessler dives, this being his first cage venture; an Ivy League college professor who was formerly a professional dive guide and tour leader; a semi-professional underwater photographer with a slightly shady but equally colorful past; and Carl, working on what will become his fifth underwater book.

Port Lincoln, South Australia. Departure point for a Great White photo safari.

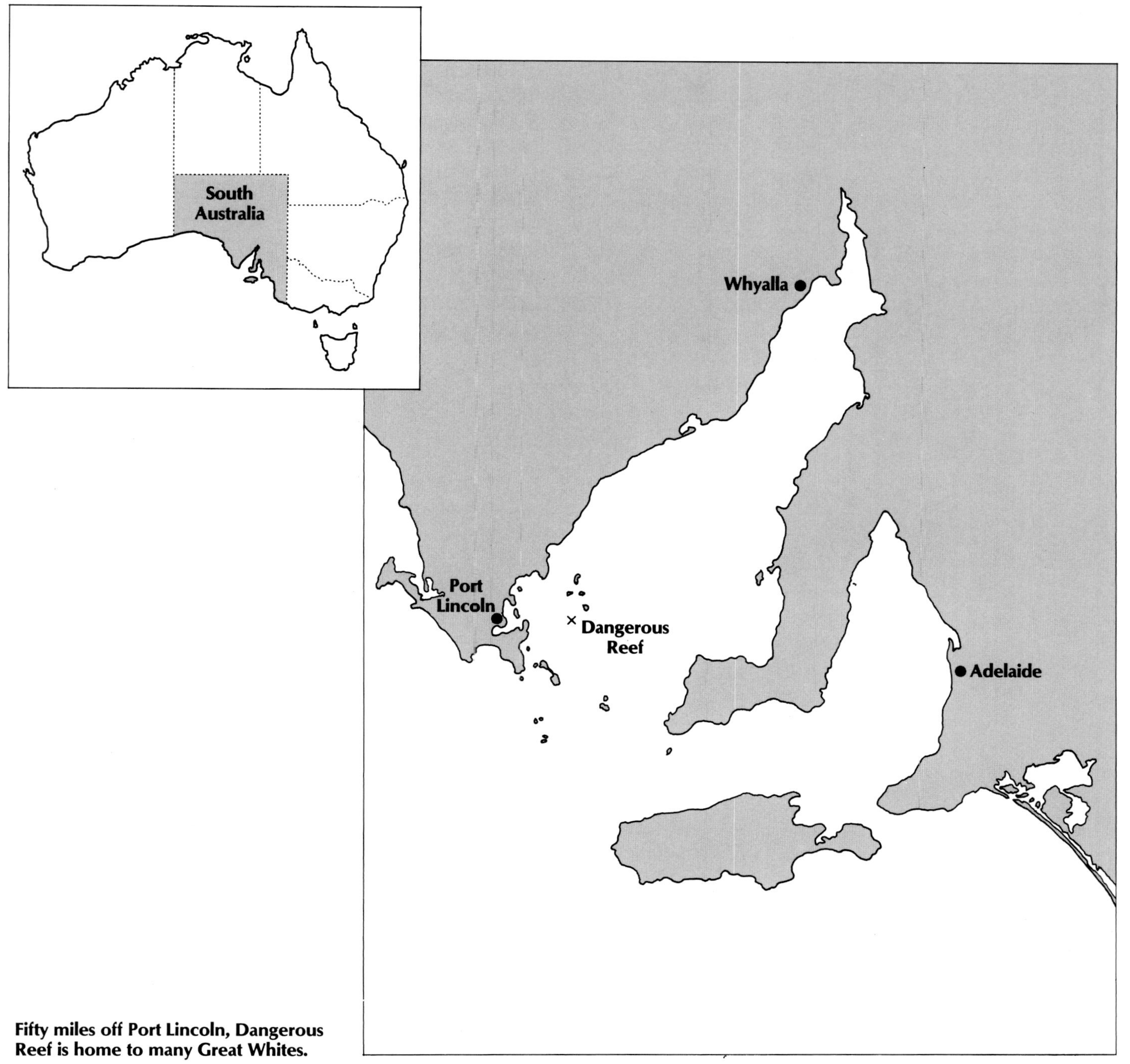

Fifty miles off Port Lincoln, Dangerous Reef is home to many Great Whites.

Day One

EVERYONE ARRIVES AT PORT Lincoln, a small town at the tip of South Australia. You're met at the airport by the staff of the boat you'll be on; the luggage—mounds of it—is gathered and stuffed into assorted trucks and cars. A short drive later you're all checking into a local motel for the night prior to the next day's putting out to sea.

There's a change of plans, though, and the "rest" lasts only a few hours instead of overnight. The weather is beginning to act up, and the crew members, who know the skies as well as you know your commute route back home, decide that unless the boat leaves right away the channel run to the open ocean will be more than everyone would care to deal with. Did you bring your Dramamine pills or Scopolamine patch? You don't mind the switch in schedule, however, since all of you are anxious to get to Great White country as soon as possible.

From this point on, Rodney Fox, one of the world's most liked and respected authorities on the White Shark, is in charge. He'll be aided by his son Andrew, just in his early twenties and already a veteran diver and shark guide.

The two of them have spent many days collecting the twenty or so buckets of "chum"—blood, fish oils, tuna and frozen chunks of both fish and meat. This, says Rodney—who conducts three to five such trips each year, mostly for filmmakers and researchers—is the hardest part.

The crew consists of the highly experienced captain, an assistant plus a cook—all men who are regularly professional shrimp fishers, but who use this off-season time to their financial advantage. The week before your group arrived, the boat and this same crew had escorted the film staff of television's "Wild Kingdom" on a similar hunt; for two weeks before that, they hosted a photographer and assistants from *National Geographic* magazine. It's been a busy off-season, and will probably be even busier next year as more and more scientists and recreational divers decide to experience a few brief moments in the life of the Great White Shark—the ultimate predator in its own environment.

You're shown below, to the windowless square room that usually serves as the storage compartment for the fish nets. A few feet off the floor, door-sized planks have been braced along the walls as bunks for you and the other divers. People stash their photo and personal gear at the foot of their bunks, in corners of the room, and on a makeshift table erected along one wall. The scuba equipment is left in the individual dive bags on deck where each of you have commandeered a couple of square feet of personal space amidst the coiled hoses and lines needed for washing down the decks and hoisting the cages in and out of the water.

Soon enough, as the clouds continue building, you're inside sitting around the galley's tiny table, getting to know the people with whom you'll be sharing what you hope will prove to be the most amazing week of your diving life. Whenever divers gather for the first time, there are all the questions about sites you've been to, people you know in common, new pieces of equipment someone brought, unusual animals you've seen underwater and problem scuba experiences you barely survived. This first day is no exception. And while all the conversation is interesting, and provides a needed ice-breaker for the trip, you can't help but feel that much of the talk is merely masking anxiety that is building within each of you.

An hour has slipped by unnoticed, but as the boat is now rocking significantly, you understand that the captain knew what he was talking about. You venture outside on deck and see increasingly rough water ahead. You've never been seasick before, but you realize that the trip may hold more "firsts" than you anticipated. Maybe a nap is in order.

It doesn't help. A couple of hours later you're back topside, a sour taste in your throat and a slippery feeling in your stomach.

Somehow you manage, and later even get down some of the first night's meal of sandwiches and snacks. Tomorrow will be better, won't it?

Custom-made steel shark cages are positioned on deck.

Day Two

WHILE YOU'VE BEEN, MUCH TO your amazement, comfortably asleep, the boat has been making its way to Dangerous Reef, the locale of much of the live footage seen in "Jaws" and "Blue Water, White Death." You're relieved to hear a crew member tell someone else that the reef got its name decades ago—in the days of the seafarers—when ships piled upon it during storms.

In the morning the "slick" is started when Rodney, almost ceremoniously, pours the first ladle of chum over the side. All the divers will take turns scooping the red blood mixed with fish oil, so that every ten minutes the slick will be added to, laying a wide path of oil on top of the water. The wave action will carry it miles out to sea. There, it's hoped, a cruising Great White will intersect it and follow the slick upcurrent back to the boat.

You're told that it may be a day or more before you see a shark, but still you find yourself staring over the ocean by the hour, hoping against reality that you'll spot that famous fin sliding through the surface of the water. Meanwhile, there's more talk with the other divers, learning where they came from, about their families and careers, yet knowing inside that all this is simply a diversion—all of you, really, are thinking about the same single things: Will you find sharks, when, and what will it be like when you get in that cage for the first time; will you be frightened, will anything go wrong; will you come away with decent pictures; will all this be worth the trouble, time, and expense?

You've brought a handful of books, mostly about the sea or scuba diving or adventure, but you can't manage to relax enough yet to settle in some corner with one. Instead, you dig through your dive bag, looking over gear you studied at least five times at home in preparation. You're not really accomplishing anything, though the action does seem to help ease the nerves and provide a valuable preamble to the events that lie ahead. You're priming the pump, as it were.

More ladles of chum add to the slick that stretches past the horizon.

Rodney Fox adds to the "slick" in a big way. Right, bagged and loose fish scraps leach oils continuously.

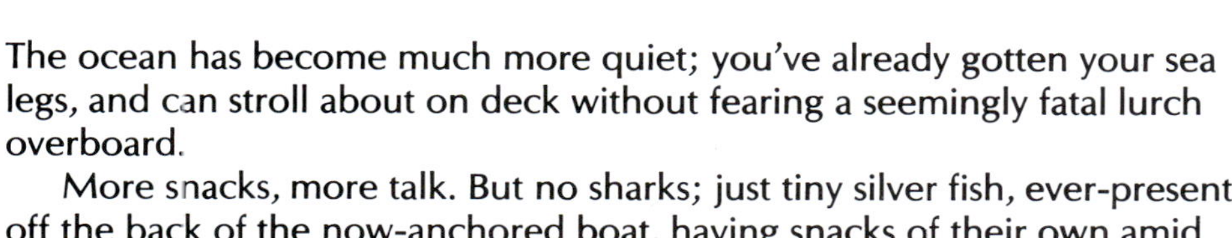

The ocean has become much more quiet; you've already gotten your sea legs, and can stroll about on deck without fearing a seemingly fatal lurch overboard.

More snacks, more talk. But no sharks; just tiny silver fish, ever-present off the back of the now-anchored boat, having snacks of their own amid the chum and its flecks of minced tuna. There are jokes about going for a swim, anecdotes about "Jaws," tales of life in Australia—and a few more hours sneak past.

The brightly yellow sun begins setting, and you feel like it's time to hit the bunk. It's hours before your normal bedtime, but you're ready nonetheless. An excellent seafood dinner, and you vanish below unnoticed for a little reading; very little, as it turns out, since you're sound asleep within minutes.

Day Three

ALL YESTERDAY AND TODAY, nothing. You're fifty miles out to sea, on deck, tiptoeing around what seems like miles of ropes and hoses on this sixty-five foot temporarily-converted shrimper, wondering if this was such a hot idea after all.

Where are the "stars" of this truly unique dive trip? Some of you, maybe only partially in jest, laugh about tossing old Roessler overboard to see what turns up. Carl, too, laughs, but less robustly.

By now the waiting game is looking more like a waning game. Not only have you relaxed and gotten into reading, you're actually through your first book and halfway into number two. Your tan is improving, you tell yourself, looking on the positive side. You've gotten headaches squinting toward the reflecting ocean in search of the elusive fin; you've asked all the Australian-related questions you can think of; and you don't care any longer about people's favorite dive spots. In fact, you may hate to admit it when you get back home, but you've taken to watching TV! Yep, television in the galley, some Australian-held international soccer playoff—and you don't even like soccer.

More chum; at least it's something to do, and you feel like you're trying, in some minuscule way, to help things along. Hell, what else can you do besides wait and hope? How are you ever going to answer when friends ask you what the Great Whites were like?

Another fine dinner, another early bedtime, and a second book finished. At this rate, you tell yourself, you could get through the *Encyclopaedia Brittanica* before boarding the return flight.

You drift off, to be awakened during the night for your regular watch, and dumping that nasty glop in the water every ten minutes. At first you poured the chum in with confident anticipation, now you dump it over the side with an automatic disregard as the small Tommy Ruffs attack the goo as it hits the water. What started out as "chum," is now simply "goo."

Where is the danger? Where is the adrenalin rush? Where, for God's sake, are the sharks? To bed. Maybe tomorrow . . .

Day Four

MORE OF THE SAME THIS morning, so far. You've been up scanning the surface since seven, and now it's after ten.

"Shack! Shack!," Rodney yells in his heavy Australian accent. It takes you some seconds to realize what he's saying, that a White, the first of what you dearly hope will be many, has shown up. You rush, stumbling around supply boxes, dive gear, and those damn ropes, to the stern—and there it is. The first Great White you've ever seen is making slow, almost studied passes near the foot-square meat chunk that floats ten feet away tied to the boat by nylon rope. The shark is barely under the surface of the jade-colored water, its dorsal fin in the air—exactly as in the movies, exactly as in your dreams.

Roessler and Rodney can relax for the moment. They got you a White.

Everyone lends a hand, attaching the two shark cages, one at a time, to the winch which will swing them out to each side to be lowered slowly into the water. A crew member keeps the shark in the vicinity with more cups of chum and a couple of small baits, not wanting the shark to fill up right away and leave. White Sharks don't simply eat endlessly; when they're content, off they go, not to be seen for a day or even weeks, and you don't want that.

The cages float at the surface, hanging downward about eight feet into the water. At the top are two wire doors for divers' entrance and exit. The sides are interwoven 1/4" steel rods that all of a sudden look precariously fragile. The floor, too, is the same wire fencing; once in the cage you'll learn to hook your toes under a couple of those rods to steady yourself against ocean swells and shark bumps. Each cage also features a more open viewing area through which you can see the animals without feeling you're behind bars. It's out these openings, too, that you'll reach with your camera as you get braver, hoping for that one perfect shark photo.

Not everyone is immediately set for their first cage plunge, but Carl, who has done this five or six times before, is already in his 1/4" wet suit, a

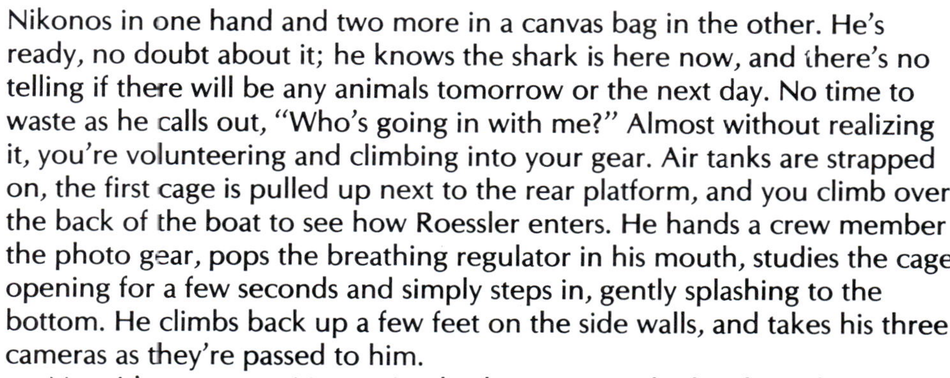

Nikonos in one hand and two more in a canvas bag in the other. He's ready, no doubt about it; he knows the shark is here now, and there's no telling if there will be any animals tomorrow or the next day. No time to waste as he calls out, "Who's going in with me?" Almost without realizing it, you're volunteering and climbing into your gear. Air tanks are strapped on, the first cage is pulled up next to the rear platform, and you climb over the back of the boat to see how Roessler enters. He hands a crew member the photo gear, pops the breathing regulator in his mouth, studies the cage opening for a few seconds and simply steps in, gently splashing to the bottom. He climbs back up a few feet on the side walls, and takes his three cameras as they're passed to him.

Now it's your turn. No turning back. You were the hotshot who piped up at the first call. And it's time. Carl, beneath the surface and already preparing his camera equipment, has moved to the other side of the cage, leaving you a clear entry. With the regulator in your mouth you don't need to hold your breath, but instinctively you do. As you step off the boat you hear yourself saying, "Here goes nothing." You're in the cage, bouncing lightly off the bottom as you land, bubbles everywhere. Well, your first entry wasn't exactly a scene from "Swan Lake," but you didn't look like a fool, either.

For this once-in-a-lifetime trip you bought an additional Nikonos, and borrowed a third. You have a super wide angle 15mm lens on one camera, a 28mm on another and a 35mm on the third. But with all the anxiety of this first shark, this first cage, you left them topside. You realize this as Rodney pushes the cage away with a long pole so the White Shark won't be shied off by the boat.

Recent rough weather, plus a good half-bucket of chum, have made the water murkier than you'd expected. The visibility is perhaps just ten or fifteen feet. For the shark, however, it's quite a bit more. Because you are so near the surface, a single tank of air will last much longer than it would at, say, a hundred feet. This first cage experience of your life will last more than three hours, and when you come out your muscles will ache from the cold. Even with your 1/4" wetsuit, three hours in fifty-five degree water takes its toll.

But while you're in the cage, body temperature is the last thing on your mind. In fact, the three hours will seem like forty-five minutes, because as your eyes and senses acclimate to this new environment, you realize that there isn't just one shark, nor are there two; you have three Great Whites on your first day in the water—and here you are without a camera. From the corner of your eye you notice Roessler, cameras everywhere. The rat. No matter. You've come to experience this perfect animal in its own surroundings. Photos would be great, but for now they are secondary to the realization that you're looking virtually eye-to-eye with one of the great wonders of the living world, an animal feared by all, one considered to be a perfect creature given its purpose, and one that has remained unchanged in all basic ways for so many millions of years. Awe inspiring, that's what it is. And there you are.

Your cage is seven feet wide by five feet, so as the sharks glide by, you can estimate their sizes. The smallest appears to be nine feet, another about thirteen and the third, *fourteen*. Amazing. Three-quarters the length of a Sherman Tank.

To keep the Whites around, crewmen occasionally toss healthy cups full of blood over the top of the cage, filling your view with the most gorgeous color of red you've ever seen. Never mind that it's blood and whale oil, and never mind that you better wash that wetsuit well when you get back home. The chum disperses into the water, giving the sharks a teasing smell of what they hope they'll soon find. Before the cage was lowered away, baits of twenty-pound meat were tied to the top bars so they'd float eight or ten feet away from the cage. To the shark, Roessler estimates, the cage, even with people in it, probably appears as a monolithic block—an impenetrable mass to swim around rather than try to swim through. This is why, perhaps, the Whites never really *attack* the cage trying to get after the potential meal inside.

So, for most of those first two hours, the White Sharks simply "stroll" around their neighborhood, checking things out. Baits go ignored. But at hour three everything changes. For the prior half-hour you two have been alone in the cage, no sounds but your air bubbles, no sights but the six-inch Tommy Ruffs that will be your persistent companions the entire trip as they swim around the boat feasting on the particles of the chum. They don't seem to be at all phased by the massive and deadly sharks, probably knowing the Whites aren't the least bit interested in anything so tiny. You start to think that the sharks may have gotten bored and left for the day,

Tommy Ruffs surround the cage,
feasting on flecks of chum.

and find yourself checking your air gauge for the first time. How could it be that you still have so much air? Because you're so near the surface, you remind yourself.

The two of you are still searching the steel-blue water, though, hoping to spot a tail in the distance. You stand back-to-back, being certain that all vistas are covered. You've already developed the signals for when one spots a White—a swift backward kick does nicely.

"Crunch!" What's that! Right above you, at the upper corner of the cage, is the biggest mouth you've ever imagined. A White is chomping away at the bars just inches from your head. Instinctively you duck. Foolish, but you can't help it. You remember Carl, and flail your left leg behind you wildly. No need, though, he's recognized that sound, whirled around and fired half a roll of film before you've recovered your balance. Seconds later the shark has withdrawn to glide silently away as if nothing had happened. Did this really take place? Did you truly see that reddened flesh of the mouth, those huge triangular teeth? No time to wonder much, though, because from nowhere there's another one biting at your lower corner. The sound is as vivid as the sight. You even see a couple of teeth break off and flutter downward into the dark.

Then they're gone again. Just like that. Were these two White Sharks trying to get an intriguing meal? Not likely. They didn't actually attack, didn't churn up the water. They just went "Chomp, chomp." Of course; they don't have arms and hands to reach and check out this strange metal object. They used what sensors they had, their nose, mouth and teeth. You wonder what thoughts went through their small brains. And, too, you remember that metal in saltwater gives off a magnetic field, and sharks instinctively respond.

You return to the boat, exhilarated but exhausted. Tired from the nervous tension of your first White Shark encounter, tired from the cold, and tired from hours of intent searching in the dull water. Others had gone into the second cage, but have also come out, and now you're hearing fish stories such as you've never heard before. "I thought he was gonna take the camera right out of my hand." "Did you hear that guy munching away?" It goes on for a good hour, and you've got a couple of items to toss into the verbal stew, yourself. Throughout all this excitement, Rodney is unobtrusively continuing to lay the slick, a cup at a time.

There are two more Whites in the afternoon cage session, after which you're prepared to sleep like a bear in hibernation. However, you've been given the 3 a.m. to 4 a.m. nightwatch. At three, you'll be awakened by the man on the previous shift and ease out of your platform bed onto the floor of the windowless lower room that once housed shrimp nets and now serves as a bunkroom for the six of you. Above, you'll stare into the darkness, which is broken only by beams from the halogens high on the mast. They throw a soft, but bright circle of light onto the water at the back of the boat where you stand watch, tossing a couple of cups of goo into the water every ten minutes. Two nights later, you'll see one of the most eerie sights of the entire voyage—in the stillness of the late night hours, a twelve-footer glides just under the surface, out of the dark and into the light, to circle under the stern and ever so slowly back around again, occasionally taking a gentle nip at the side of the boat. Ghostlike, that's what it is. And so beautiful, so at ease. Just sticking around for breakfast.

At 4:10 a.m., you're back in that firm but toasty bed, worried that you won't be able to get back to sleep. That's the last thought you have until morning.

Day Five

CAN YOU POSSIBLY HAVE A better shark day than yesterday? Doubtful, but you sure hope so. The second cage session yesterday, you'd remembered the cameras, but weren't at all sure about all those *f*-stops, shutter speeds and films. Today, you're ready. And so are the White Sharks. But not right away.

It's nearly eleven, and no one has seen a sign of "Fluffy," as Roessler calls him. Andrew is standing barefoot on the rear platform at the water's surface, lazily tossing a rope with bait on it and hauling it in to see if he can attract guests. You're standing on the boat deck next to him, your land camera hanging by your side, daydreaming about yesterday's exhilarating events. Suddenly, from underneath the boat, a giant shark head roars out of the water to bite ferociously at the metal platform a scant six inches from Andrew's foot. The lad, a hefty six-footer, can move rather quickly when so motivated. "They're back!" he yells, and the rest of the group materialize on deck.

Wetsuits, tanks, cages and cameras—it's almost an automatic sequence by now. The cages had been brought out of the water before yesterday's dinner so they wouldn't bang against the boat during the night. It won't be more than ten minutes before both cages and all six divers are in the water for round two.

Last night you'd told yourself that even if you didn't sight another shark the rest of the trip, that day would have made it all worthwhile. But, you're starting to get greedy. More sharks. More, that's all you can think about as you wait in the water to see what happens next. This time, with the other cage thirty or so feet away but still clearly visible, you have a new perspective, and when the sharks do come back you're as fascinated by the scenes unfolding over there as you are by those right in front of you.

You watch how the other men react when a huge White lunges for the bait right next to their cage. Even though they're experienced divers and photographers, they instinctively withdraw into the cage—maybe only a few inches, and maybe only for a second, but they still withdraw—

especially when the shark hits unexpectedly. Do you do the same? Without a doubt. The element of surprise is there, certainly, but the *power* is almost more than you can deal with. From deep within you, from millions of years of survival instinct in your gene pool, you react.

But then there's that camera to put between you and reality for a few inches of objective response, settling the unrecognized nervousness that lies within.

By now you've learned to take your wide angle camera and simply point it toward the action, rather than sight through the viewer, remembering what Carl told you about the animal appearing farther away than it really is. A dangerous optical phenomenon at times like these. And you've learned to wave your camera toward passing sharks, hoping the reflection from the lens would get their attention. You also learned how to stick your arm and camera out of the cage for those dramatic barless closeups—after carefully looking left and right and up and down in case your shark has an unseen friend.

And you've learned why you were advised to bring that 15mm lens: When the shark comes in close you can include the entire body; but for closer shots, without getting any nearer to those teeth than is safe, your other lenses are fine.

The water's a little rougher today, and keeping yourself steady for clear photos is a little tricky. Toes tucked through the floor wires certainly helps, but you still have to lean into the cage walls to brace yourself even further. Stomach's a little loose, but no real problem, at least not yet. Fortunately, as the sea grows more active, the light grows more dim, and it's time to get back on board.

You're out of the cage, out of your wetsuit, out of film and out of energy. It's been another great day studying and photographing the Great White Shark. Tomorrow? Maybe nothing. But, maybe something special.

Taking a chance for the "perfect" shot, while hoping your subject hasn't an unseen friend nearby.

Days Six & Seven

YESTERDAY IT WAS DETERMINED that the group has seen at least six different Great Whites so far, and you've all had more activity than could ever be expected on these trips. The last couple of days are no exception. From morning to night cages and divers are in the water. Sharks aren't working the cages all the time, though. They come in, give a show for an hour, then glide away for thirty or forty minutes, returning for more bait, more photographs. Divers climb out only when they've exhausted themselves or their film supply, the last hardy souls giving up when the light is simply too dim for picture taking.

You're onboard in the galley having lunch when the captain, who was resting on the stern, yells that there's a monster out there! Two guys are still in a cage, but they're floating on the port side while the real action is off the starboard. Four of you and Rodney stare into the water in disbelief at the biggest shark of all—maybe fifteen feet long and perhaps a ton-and-a-half. It makes two passes toward the boat, then seems to dive under. You're prepared this time, your land camera cocked and at the ready as you rush to the opposite side to get the shot as the creature comes up and breaks the surface. You poise, knowing that at any second you'll have an opportunity for photographic immortality. Then, from behind, you hear shouts and screams. You whip around automatically to see the White Shark vertical in the air, on eye-level with the men standing there in near terror.

"My God! It came right at me!"

"Did you see that? It stared right at us, chomped three times at the air, and fell back."

"Unbelievable."

"Did you get the shot?" Rodney excitedly asks you. "It'd be the picture of a lifetime."

Well, not exactly. You were prepared, though. Just on the wrong side of the boat, that's all. How could you be so unlucky, you wonder to yourself, such a wimp? For the next few minutes the fact that you've already taken more than 400 photos is dreadfully unimportant.

This giant of a White goes on to molest the cage that contains the other two divers, giving them photos and experiences they'll never forget. Then it leaves. It never took a bait.

Later this final afternoon, it's agreed that Carl and Rodney want to try something different; they want to flood the air tubes on one of the cages so it'll sink forty feet to sands below. Again you volunteer. A signal rope will be attached to the side of the cage while Andrew holds the other end onboard. One tug means to lower the cage more, two means pull it up a bit, and three means to haul it back to the surface. You'll see the sharks from a very rare vantage point, from below, and without baits to create artificial reactions.

The three of you suit up, put on the tanks and jump into the cage. Carl and Rodney reach up to open valves on the floats. As the floats fill with sea water, the cage begins its gradual descent. You land gently on the sand, and just as gently the cage falls over on its side. Disorienting, to say the least. A couple of tugs on the rope and you're back up off the bottom; another tug and you're lowered again, this time remaining upright.

You've got two sharks immediately. The twelve-foot one you recognize from scratches on its side, perhaps from the cages or even the boat's hull. The other is younger, smaller, and new to the three of you. They meander around the area, paying absolutely no attention to the cage. They don't even come near. Perhaps as a fixture on the sand, the cage simply isn't noticed as something of interest. You shoot a roll of film, realizing that you're capturing scenes few people have ever witnessed—White sharks at the ocean floor, and more than one in each picture which you can't recall ever seeing in books.

While all this is captivatingly new to you, Roessler and Fox want something more. You look up to see them open the cage top to climb halfway out for better views, better pictures and better thrills. They check their camera settings and, scanning in all directions, they wait. For the first ten minutes the sharks couldn't care less about these two silly creatures. And then a third, even larger one, enters the scene. Right away, with no preamble, no warning, it heads right for Rodney. You're too stunned, too afraid of what you might see right above you, to use your camera. Hell, you're not a combat photographer, you're a tourist on vacation. Good lord, Rodney's going to get it again!

But he doesn't. As casually as if he were pushing an unwanted dog off a porch, Fox uses his camera to nonchalantly shove the Great White Shark in the face, making it pass overhead. An arm's length away, 2,000 pounds and thirty or more teeth were aiming straight at Rodney Fox. Then, bump, and it's gone past. You stare in disbelief. You realize you are starting to shiver. Must be that fifty-five degree water. Maybe.

Forty minutes later, you've got your shots and your excitement for the day. And Rodney has another good story to tell.

Day Eight

TIME TO GO. ONE LAST STOP, though. You motor to one of the tiny islands along Dangerous Reef, one inhabited by thousands of sea lions; pups, mothers and bulls. This, of course, is why researchers know to come here when they want to look for sharks. With the pinnipeds in and out of the water all day, it's a virtual White Shark's smorgasbord.

You're in the first group that takes the small boat (the "tinny" to the Australians) to the island. You're instructed to stay downwind so the animals will be less aware of you, to stay bent low so you don't intimidate the bulls by appearing larger than them and not to get too near the pups if there's a mother close by. You shoot a couple more rolls, getting totally caught up in the beauty of the females and the cuteness (there's really no more apt word) of the babies, forgetting for the moment that they are what your magical white eminence lives on.

Hours later, you arrive at Port Lincoln and disembark to share in the hauling of the gear up to the dock. This time it's easier, though. No huge packs of chopped ice to keep the chum cold, no more full buckets, and no more sacks of frozen meat for Fluffy. Rodney admits that this is the first trip he can recall when there was so much shark activity that every piece of bait onboard was used up.

You all check into the local motel for the night, and you can hear the showers running in the adjacent rooms for a very long time. After nearly an hour, you emerge from your own, wrinkled but refreshed. There's a mini-banquet later where all of you, plus the crew and a few wives, have a glorious champagne dinner, with more than enough funny toasts and more than enough great food.

You go to bed with mixed feelings: You're glad to be on your way back to home and family, but depressed that you'll probably never experience the Great White Shark the same way again; happy that you don't have the 3 a.m. watch tonight, but worried that none of your photos will come out. Then you turn over and are asleep in an instant.

CHAPTER THREE

The Ultimate Shark

CARCHARODON CARCHARias. That's what scientists call the White Shark. In Australia, it's termed a White Pointer; in South Africa it's a Blue Pointer; and in Hawaii, those who can, call it a Mano Ni-uhi. There's also White Death and other equally dramatic names. Generally, "Great White" will get the message across.

The Great White Shark is, though, only one of those 350-plus identified shark types. We all must keep this in mind; it is a small corner of a very large picture, one element in a vast chain of sea life. But, while it's true that this "ultimate shark" is just one of many, it's a very special one.

The White Shark—one of only twenty species that has been known to attack humans—normally reaches up to twenty feet. Researchers in cages generally find that the creatures they're looking at range from ten to fifteen feet. Some sources claim the largest documented find to have been a twenty-one footer caught off Cuba in the Thirties; its weight was estimated at 7,000 pounds. There are stories, perhaps true, of one in Hawaii fifty years ago being thirty-nine feet long. The British Museum of Natural History boasts a reconstructed jaw of a White that would have reached more than thirty-six feet, though today's experts are rather skeptical since the scientific process in the mid-1800s in the shark field was haphazard at best. (This "monster jaw," usually shown with a handful of stern-looking scientists perched formally inside, was reconstructed based on one actual tooth.) There is another claim, perhaps worth more merit, of presumably the largest White Shark accurately measured. This one, identified in 1935 by Dr. Vadim Vladyker, was a thirty-seven footer trapped accidentally in a fish net at White Head Island, New Brunswick, Canada.

In 1959, Australian Alf Dean, a legendary shark hunter, established a rod and reel fish record. His 130-pound-test line hauled in a 16′10″ Great White that weighed 2,664 pounds. It was twenty-seven years before Dean's rod and reel catch was bettered, this time by Dennis Braddick off Montauk, Long Island, New York. Guided by the well-known sharker Frank Mundas, Braddick used a 150-pound-test nylon line to catch a 3,450 pound seventeen-footer—

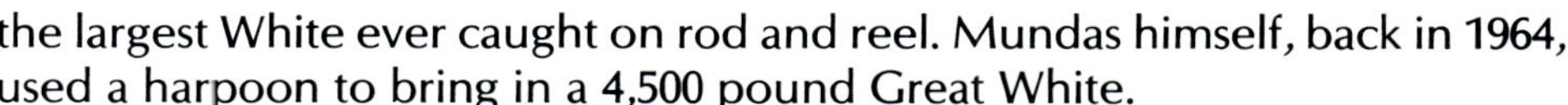

the largest White ever caught on rod and reel. Mundas himself, back in 1964, used a harpoon to bring in a 4,500 pound Great White.

Generally, though, most large Great Whites average fourteen to fifteen feet in length, and weigh in at around 1,200 to 2,000 pounds. The young are developed from eggs within the female, and are born at about fifty inches and a hundred pounds. Now, either they grow to their massive size very rapidly, or they take many years; we simply don't know.

But this is only one of the many gaps in our knowledge of this captivating fish. You'd think that a creature who has been on this earth virtually unchanged for 400,000,000 years would have few secrets. Not the case. We know almost nothing about its longevity, its age at maturity, its regular locale or travel patterns, mating behavior, growth rate and so much more. When you realize that we can't accurately estimate how many there are or how large they grow, you can understand part of the reason the Great White has an "image" problem. When knowledge is absent, fear fills in the blanks.

The difficulties in gathering data on Whites are many. Whites roam most of the ocean's temperate waters, and exist from depths of a few feet to more than 4,000'—at least. They don't survive in captivity, so can't be

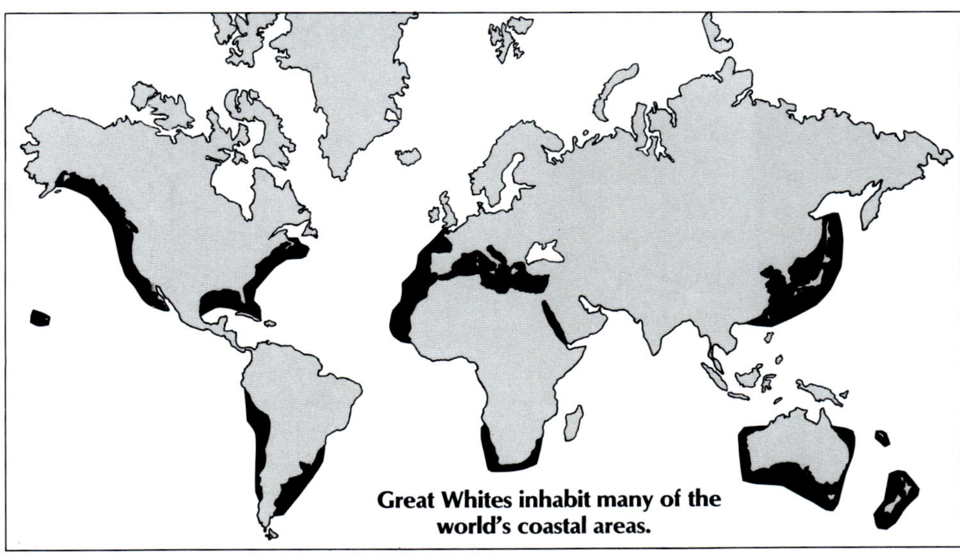

Great Whites inhabit many of the world's coastal areas.

studied in the usual ways, and their natural environment is the entire sea. When they die, at whatever age that might be, their bodies sink to the bottom to simply decay, leaving only the teeth (they have no bones). The biggest Whites caught have been brought up accidentally in nets by fishermen who must number among the most surprised people on earth at the time. However, how many tuna boats can haul a twenty-five foot Great White around? And if they could, what fish-weighing gear can deal with a ton of shark? So, often the creature is devoured by other fish while being towed to harbor, and weight just has to be guessed at.

It's because of this acknowledged lack of information concerning these fascinating animals, that scientists and researchers have begun serious cage work over the past decade. It's probable, though, that in the past ten years, fewer than fifteen cage trips have been run to investigate the Great White Shark, and it's estimated that less than one hundred people have gone down to watch, test, photograph, and take notes. But the interest is growing, certainly, and the next decade should yield more data than has all the rest of history's research to date.

How do you know when you're eye-to-eye with a White and not one of the other 349 varieties? If you enjoy flirting with the gods you can check out the teeth. Those of the White are clearly triangular and have serrated edges. These saw blades can easily cut through two-inch nylon rope, so you can imagine the damage they can cause to flesh and bone. The teeth range from one to three inches, but are only loosely embedded in the gums, with the result that they can easily shatter or break off if the shark bites into, say, a metal shark cage, or the side of a boat. Not to worry, though; the White has a virtual conveyor belt in its mouth, so that other teeth lie flat right behind the frontal ones, just waiting to rotate forward in a few days. It's been said that Whites' teeth are replaced regularly every six to twelve months.

The most obvious physical characteristic, though, is the White's conical snout, explaining why many people call the animal a "pointer." This is in clear contrast to the much more common flat head we see in aquarium sharks. The eye, too, is distinctive; it has no visible pupil, but is instead, a solid black disc—seemingly unchanging and unmoving. The eyes do have one mobile trait; they can roll back in their sockets as protection right at the moment the shark bites its prey. Scientists speculate that this ability

The teeth of the Great White, and many other sharks, are loosely embedded in the jaw, while others lie back as ready replacements.

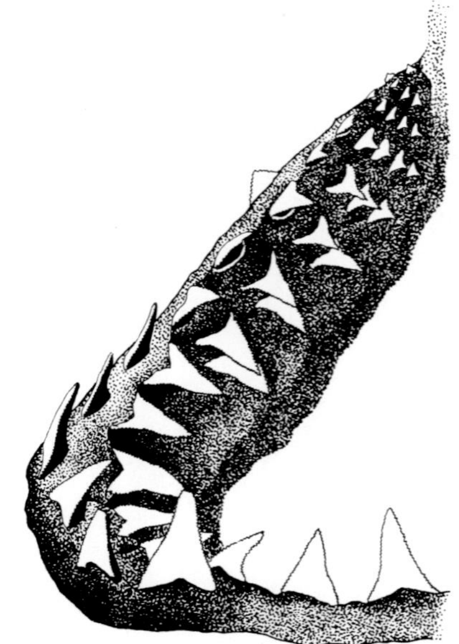

Approximate Maximum Sizes

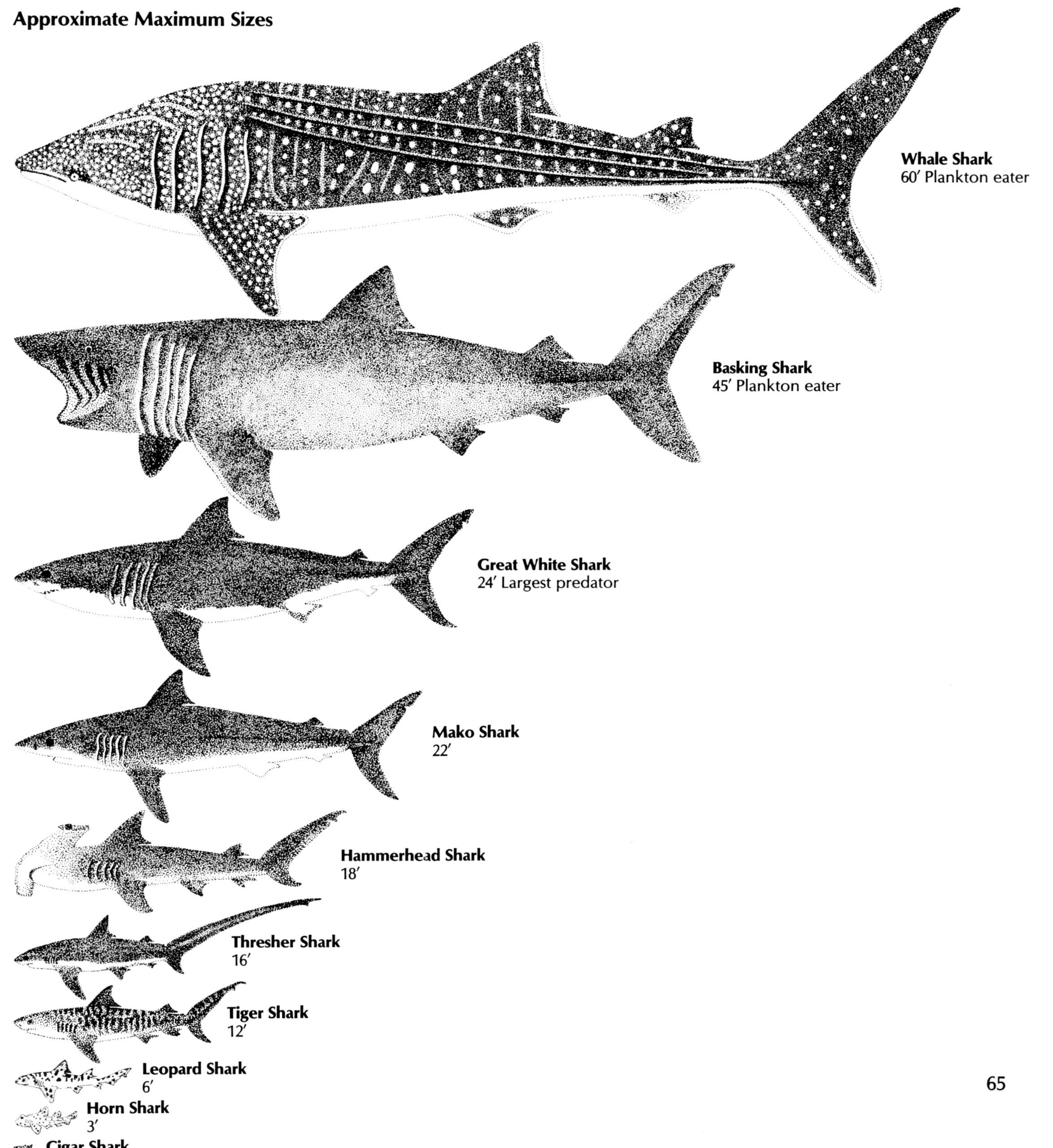

DRAWINGS BY KATHY GOLDEN

protects this most vulnerable part of the creature when it bites, say, sea lions with their dangerously sharp claws.

The Great White isn't totally white, so you can also recognize it by a distinct line of demarcation along the sides where its lower pale white skin joins the upper dark gray or even gray-brown half. A seal, for instance, looking up toward the brighter surface and sky, would see only a vague, light shape, and perhaps not notice that this was a White Shark; similarly, a porpoise near the top of the water might glance down toward the darkening bottom and not recognize the gray outline circling in the vicinity.

In addition, Whites have black coloring at the tips of their pectoral fins. Some also have a black spot where the pectoral fins join the body. There are other, more subtle differences, too, but if you're capable of recognizing them, you already know them. The coloration, the conical snout, the triangular teeth—if you see those, get back in the boat.

What is your chance of encountering a Great White in the ocean? Little or none. For one thing, the ocean is a rather big place, naturally, and the Whites are relatively rare. Sure, you can intentionally search out the creature in places where it's most common—such as a dozen miles out of the San Francisco Bay in California, or fifty miles off Port Lincoln in South Australia. But Hollywood would have us believe that the shark may even be in our backyard pools.

White Sharks come close to shore only occasionally. In 1985 in South Australia the ultimate fear became a reality. A husband and wife with their four children were spending a day at Wiseman's Beach. The woman, snorkeling in six feet of water about 150 yards offshore, was bit in two by a Great White. This was the first attack in those waters in six years, and one of the most brutal imaginable. Was this a "maneater," a crazed animal set upon wanton destruction? Or, perhaps, was the shark simply doing what it does—eat—and poor Shirley Ann Durdin was in the wrong place at the wrong time? There was a fishing festival happening at that time, and thousands of pounds of fish cleanings were being dumped into those same waters emitting the scent of food. Might these innocent fishermen have had some unwitting responsibility for this most horrible of events?

But back to the question of whether or not you'll ever see a Great White at sea. We know they exist worldwide, primarily in temperate or tropical waters. In the middle of the 18th century they were spotted even as far north as the British Isles. However, consider that these same oceans are visited by untold millions of bathers, swimmers, surfers, and board sailors every day of the year. And remember, the White will come right up to the shoreline if it wants. But do you personally know anyone who has ever seen one? The number who have is relatively infinitesimal.

Throughout the world, there are only thirty to fifty non-fatal attacks recorded annually. Granted, one attack is one too many, but the odds are clearly with you that you're a good deal safer in the water than on the freeway.

Even professional scientists, spending weeks at sea in waters known to be home to many Great Whites, have their troubles finding them. *National Geographic* has even come up empty-handed on occasion. I recall discussing one of their Australia trips with the chief underwater photographer who described his fifteen days onboard a boat, chumming the waters every hour, day and night, without a sighting. Researchers from San Francisco's Steinhart Aquarium spent similar days off Northern California's Farallon Islands, one of the most shark-infested areas of the world, dumping hundreds of pounds of meat, fish, and blood in the water, and not finding a White.

Are you safe? Sure. Up to a point. But more about that later.

The White Shark is an amazing fish in many ways. It is the ultimate combination of power and grace, violence and beauty. But it hasn't existed for millions of years on force alone. It can smell blood in the water a mile away, and can hear what's going on for a hundred yards. Its vision is equally astounding. Some authorities claim the shark has clear sight for twenty to forty feet, while others credit this ability up to a hundred feet. And this is generally in water so murky that humans can see no more than twenty feet ahead.

As you can imagine, fish the size of the average adult Great White need plenty of food. If they had to survive on what came their way during daylight hours, they'd probably have evolved to be half their present size. However, these mesmerizing eyes seem to be as acute during the night as in the day, extending the available feeding time dramatically.

The White is a warm-blooded animal, and maintains its body temperature approximately seven degrees above the surrounding water. It accom-

plishes this feat through simple muscle action, varying its temperature hourly. We do the same on cold days by shivering. Both behaviors are uncontrolled and equally effective.

But the White has an even more unique ability. Between its front tip and mouth are tiny electro-magnetic sensors called the Ampullae of Lorinzini. At a glance these small pock holes look almost like close-cut whiskers. In effect, they help the shark "see" its prey by picking up minute low-frequency electrical charges which emanate from such things as wounded fish, struggling swimmers and certain metals (this latter is why sharks have been seen to bite boat propellers and shark cages—as the metal encounters saltwater, electrolysis takes place, and the resulting magnetic field can be almost irresistible to the shark.) When the White makes that final, usually fatal, lunge at its meal, it generally cocks its head far back to protrude its mouth for the bite; at that brief moment, it can't see what's there. Enter the ampullae, which "electronically" guide the shark to its goal.

To survive in the animal world, caution is a necessary trait. The Great White Shark, even with nothing to be afraid of except man, is a perfect example of this. This massive predator doesn't rush its prey, doesn't roar its way through the water, thrashing left and right to snap at whatever comes along. It's careful, it's usually slow, and it's cooly deliberate. Uncontrolled feeding frenzies do exist among sharks, but none have been recorded with the Great White.

Instead, they prefer to circle their prey slowly if that prey is relatively motionless—say, a wounded seal, a sleeping otter, or that inattentive rare surfer. Then, when they decide to strike, the circle becomes an arc, and the shark heads right for the target.

The White is nothing if not stealthy. Downright sneaky, it usually prefers to attack from below and behind, catching its meal totally unaware. You can be in a shark cage, intently looking from one side to the other, up and down, continuously for an hour, then turn back to where you were staring a few seconds ago, and there it is. You don't know where it came from, you didn't see a hint of it in the distance. It just seemed to appear, and maybe only ten feet away.

I recall being in a cage off South Australia's Neptune Islands, tying an air tank into the cage's corner to then breathe from it through a scuba regulator. Since I had to reach outside to wrap the bungie cord around the bars

and back to the tank, I was the picture of wide-eyed caution, looking rapidly in every direction. There was nothing in front, below, left or right—until a fraction of a second after I'd brought my arm back inside. At that moment a seeming giant of a White chomped the cage right where my arm had been an instant before. Where it came from I'll never know.

The White Shark makes these sudden appearances mysteriously, almost magically. Certainly not through blinding speed. Shark authority John McCosker attached miniature "speedometers" to some of the animals in Australia. Through electronic monitoring, he concluded that Whites normally swim at only one to three miles an hour. No doubt, this is generally true. With their uncanny ability to come upon prey unseen, speed is often a useless skill, one which wastes energy and which would cause the shark to need even more food to supply that energy.

I've never seen a shark ram a cage, though a White did try to come into mine once. As usual, it made passes, slow and deliberate ones, right in front of my cage as I clicked away with the Nikonos underwater camera. But then, instead of veering away at the last second, it came straight ahead, its snout entering one of the open squares of the 1/4" steel framework. No sudden surge, no boiling water, just that two-mile-an-hour "stroll." I was stunned with surprise as I heard the bars creak in separation. Three seconds later, the White simply backed away and continued off into the blue, leaving a bent cage, and an underwater photographer who found he'd been too absorbed in what was happening to take a single shot.

All this is not to say that the Great White can't really motor when it's of a mind to. On another dive, a buddy and I were sharing a cage in rather rough water. He began to feel a bit seasick, and motioned to me that he was going to climb the side to the surface and ask to be brought back onboard. We hadn't seen sharks for nearly three hours by then, anyway, so my partner thought this a safe time to open the cage lid and call to the crew. Just as he raised the top, stuck his head above water and removed the regulator from his mouth, a fourteen-footer hit one of the baits that was tied to the cage. The creature gobbled the twenty-five pound snack in a flash, then twisted its body in an effort to break the food free of the tether. The rope, though, lodged itself deeply between two teeth, and as the shark continued to spiral, it reeled itself up against the side of the cage. It didn't take to that idea one bit. The shark thrashed us wildly from side to

Thick nylon rope used to secure the cages to the boat, and occasionally attached to chunks of bait. Almost impossible to cut with a knife, the rope offers almost no resistance to a determined White Shark.

side in its understandable fury, throwing my buddy back into the cage in complete astonishment as he madly groped for the air-giving regulator. For a few seconds I feared the shark would break our cage free of the boat and haul us under the sea. Fortunately, in its mad gyrations, it managed to saw the nylon rope through and blast away below like a shell fired from a cannon. This time, I had my photographic wits about me, however, and grabbed a couple of quick pictures—pictures, it later turned out, of brilliant white foam. Not much shark, but great foam.

So, yes the Great White is slow, very slow, unless it decides otherwise.

The stomachs of Great Whites have been known to yield all the stuff we've so often read about: bottles, boxes of canned goods and so on. However, you don't survive as long as cockroaches and scorpions by making mistakes. No, the Whites' basic diet consists primarily of sea turtles, an occasional dolphin, seals and sea lions, with otters and a few other small critters as hors d'oeuvres. If they ate smaller creatures, they'd expend too much time and energy.

Whites aren't agile enough to hunt down such lithe and speedy mammals as sea lions. Here's where stealth comes in once more. Also, the shark looks for the infirm or injured, aiding, in its way, the other species by ridding the waters of those animals which would deteriorate the breed. In these habits, sharks, particularly the White, help keep the balance of life in the sea. A true and natural environmentalist.

Above, the Normal Underwater Pass method of feeding. Right, the Side Roll manner; note the balloon to keep the bait floating near the surface for the photographers' benefit.

CHAPTER FOUR

Danger: Real Or Imagined

CERTAINLY THE GREAT WHITE is dangerous. Not that it's a crazed killer, it just eats a lot and is a giant mass of power. Should one mistake you for a seal, it simply made an error in judgment. Whites haven't consumed enough humans for their internal messages to relay that people should be a part of the regular diet. And while few in the world have seen the White Shark, undoubtedly the odds are even less for White Sharks having seen humans. A rubber-suited diver just can't possibly taste as delicious as a fresh sea lion, can it?

But even given the animal's good intentions, a White Shark bite is nasty business. Razor-sharp serrated teeth crunching down on your side with a force equaling tons per square inch will certainly do damage. Take South Australian Rodney Fox, for instance. Today, Rodney is one of the world's foremost authorities on the Great White Shark; in 1963, Rodney was its twenty-second officially recorded victim.

Fox, the 1961 South Australia Spearfishing Champion had come in second in '62, but was determined to win again in '63. In fifty feet of water Rodney went for a couple more fish when it happened. He recalls a sudden stillness in the water just before being hit on his left side, crushing his ribs, piercing the shoulder blade, ripping open his side, and circling half his back with nine tooth-inflicted slashes three or more inches long. Through a chain of almost unbelievable circumstances (recounted in Olaf Ruhen's captivating booklet *Shark: Attacks and Adventures with Rodney Fox*) Rodney found himself on an operating room table less than an hour after his mutilated, bleeding body was picked from the sea.

A year later, his physical and mental self put back together, Rodney was diving again, soon finding himself a part of the Australian National Spearfishing Championship team.

Rodney estimates that the shark that almost made him into Hamburger Helper was only a nine-footer. And, so typical in attacks on humans, the animal took only one bite. Had it chosen to feed, Ruhen's booklet would have been a lot shorter. Rodney survived as a spearfishing champion, then

Rodney Fox. Preceding page, close-up showing the Ampullae of Lorinzini, "pock-mark" sensors.

spent a few years seeking some subconscious revenge by diving to kill as many sharks as possible using a "powerhead" device that fires a shotgun shell when pressed against the fish's body. Soon, however, Fox was to realize that the White that hit him wasn't being needlessly cruel, and was only doing what it had learned to do over millennia. Sharks have a role in the ecological balance of nature, Rodney feels, and have evolved into one of the world's most beautiful and amazing creatures.

Rodney has been intentionally in the water with Great Whites more than any other person, because these days he is the leading light in the search for information about these sharks. He's been involved in White Shark underwater film projects since working on the 1970 classic, "Blue Water, White Death," and almost every year for the past decade he has organized cage dives out to sea so that scientists and the curious can experience this most breathtaking of animals.

How did you deal with the emotional scars after the event?

Rodney Fox: The healing really has a lot to do with how people treat you, how they, for instance, omit parts from their conversations. Out of the hundreds of people who talked to me right after it happened, only one, a TV interviewer, asked me what everyone wanted to know—was I going back into the water? People are afraid you can't deal with it.

I was in pretty good physical shape; I'd been playing Australian football, and such. That helped. And I had a friend, Brian Rodger, who also had been attacked by a White Shark. He was a chiropractor and an osteopath. With his guidance I was on a fresh fruit and vegetable diet, with a lot of meat as well. And, you know, a healthy body leads to a healthy mind, and helps you get through a trauma.

Coping with a return to the water must have been difficult.

About three or four months later, my wife Kay rowed me out to a reef to join fifteen or so other divers. Surrounded by these people, I speared a few fish. We weren't on scuba back then, just free diving, I had previously been able to go down more than a hundred feet, but this time, even at shallow depths, I could feel a lot of painful pressure on my wounds.

But it was around six or seven months after the attack that I saw my next shark, and it was an experience that probably could have changed the whole situation. A couple of guys had organized a spear-fishing trip to the Althorpe Islands, one of the most exciting but hard-to-get-to places in South Australia. I felt a little hollow inside, apprehensive, and this was the first time in such cases that I brought along a rod and reel, intending to stay on the boat and fish. The captain and crew got in the dinghy and headed for the islands, leaving the three of us offshore. Then I looked over the side and saw a school of Kingfishers, which we seldom find; the next thing I knew I'd gotten into my wetsuit and was in the water with my spear gun.

Then from down below came a big black thing heading up right for me like an arrow, and I realized it was a shark. I felt immediate terror in my body. I pointed my spear gun at it just in case, and was about to pull the trigger when it realized what I was. It took off in one direction and I took off in the other yelling "Shark, shark, shark!" I swam over to the other guys, but they weren't too excited or willing to leave because there were all these big fish around to spear.

My arms weren't strong enough after my attack to pull me into the boat, so I had no choice but to stay near the other divers while they speared the fish that came around. After about forty-five minutes I got over it, and even managed to spear the largest fish of the day. But had I been able to get out of the water that day I might have gone on to become a good golfer or something instead of a diver. I might never have happily returned to the sport, and been able to make my living as an abalone diver, which I did after that.

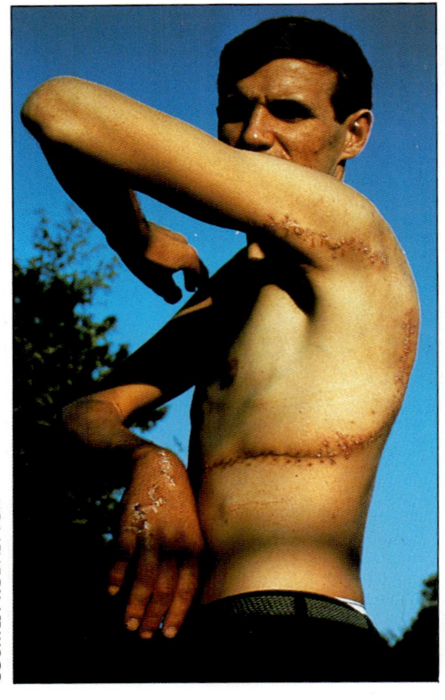

COURTESY RODNEY FOX

A few weeks after Rodney's 1963 attack by a nine-foot Great White Shark.

What would you tell someone who'd lived through a shark attack?

Most people give the White Shark more credit than it deserves, as far as thinking and planning are concerned. Actually, it's surprising how few shark attacks there really are; they're just not worth worrying about. It's like anything—in sport, business or love, people can be hurt. And in any of these you have to take whatever precautions you can.

Did you ever seriously consider never getting back into the water?

I suppose I wondered if I was going to have problems, but it really never occurred to me to quit. The previous eight years, from fifteen to twenty-three, diving was all I cared about. I spent almost every weekend

diving, saving all my money to go out. It was my life, all I ever thought about.

When did you decide to devote your life to the research and study of the Great White Shark?

In 1965 I organized the first White Shark photo expedition, and built the first cage. I took two other shark victims with me—Brian Rodger and Henri Bource—and got Ron Taylor to shoot what became the first underwater footage of the Great White Shark. Later, [producer] Peter Gimble borrowed the film to use in raising money for his movie "Blue Water, White Death."

How did you know what a shark cage should be like? Had you seen any?

No. I designed a very strong cage which, incidentally, turned out to be too strong and too heavy; it was dangerous to get in and out of the boat, in fact. I gave the shark far more ability and credit than it deserved. I used the kind of mesh you use in making concrete floors.

How many shark trips have you done?

I'm not really sure, but I've worked on twenty-seven documentaries and feature films, and maybe fifteen others with semi-professionals and other serious divers. I run about two or three a year now, not for tourists, but for such people as photographers, marine biologists and the like. To show people what these Great Whites are really about.

Do you enjoy working with filmmakers?

In the early days they were the only ones with enough money to launch such a trip and risk not seeing anything. But then they went from wanting to film all aspects of the animal to just wanting shots of biting jaws and savage sharks, which is against my goal of educating people and sharing the creature.

In more recent years we've seen greater interest on the part of such marine biologists as Eugenie Clark and John McCosker, and this started adding knowledge to the Great White Shark story. Then there have been the amateur or semi-professional photographers who started coming out, though we've often seen people who don't know about the shark stand in

Rodney, camera ready, prepares to sink below the surface.

the middle of the boat in fear that the animal will come in right over the side; after a few encounters they begin to realize the shark's limitations, and soon they're leaning over the side taking close-ups or patting the shark on the head.

We all know the effect that the film, "Jaws" had in making so many people fear the Great White Shark. Yet you accepted the role of coordinating the live-shark filming.

That's one of the things I'm not very proud of. I was asked to work on a feature film, and I was very excited to be involved in a Hollywood production. I always knew it was a fictional film; I knew these creatures didn't have the tremendous ability to think like humans. A lot of people didn't take the movie that way, and have used it as a reason not to go into the water. I think it's a disgrace.

Have your feelings about the Great White Shark changed over the years?

It's gotten to the point where you see it at the top of the chain in the shark world, the most dangerous creature in the sea, but I still feel a little sorry for them. They're a throwback to an ancient world, when their role was to cull the ocean of the diseased, the dying, the weaker animals that would otherwise breed and weaken the species. Now they're running around with nothing to do. But, over the years, I believe, the larger ones are declining. Dr. Eugenie Clark feels the females don't breed until they're about fifteen feet in length—that's approximately ten, twelve, fifteen years old. And with people catching them and killing them at that size, it's really easy to knock off the numbers quite quickly and kill off the population to the point where there won't be enough to breed.

Is there anything that can be done to prevent this?

I've been in touch with the fisheries department here in Australia, and they say it's very hard to get public opinion behind saving the Great White Shark. Elected officials find it hard to get votes if they take this position, because so many people do hate the White Shark. We have to educate the public; shark killing is such a blood sport. We have to show people that this isn't really such a dangerous animal.

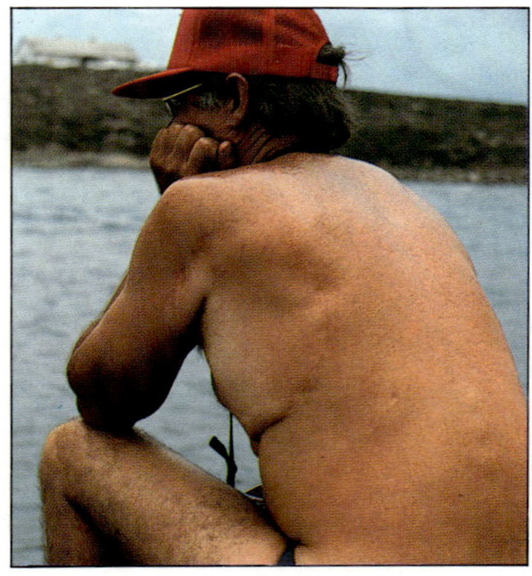

Twenty-five years later, Rodney's scars still show prominently.

Above, an old tire used as a boat bumper, usually so impregnable to damage, after a casual testing nip by a White Shark. Left, the Underwater Approach attack posture—the protruding upper jaw enlarges the bite's range when the head is arched back at the last second.

But I've noticed over the years, in newspapers, that there is less willingness to capitalize on the killing of sharks, that people feel pity when seeing photos of a dead shark hanging from a rope. With education, more and more people come out against wiping the sharks out, understanding that the animal does have a place in the world. We just can't go on killing everything.

I'm a little worried, though. I feel bad that I've played a role in causing so much more publicity for the Great White Shark than it otherwise would have. Now there are even consortiums going out after them. I'm going to continue working to get the story of these animals across to the people.

It's incredible to think that we can go to the moon, and do all these wonderful things, but concerning the largest dangerous shark in the water we don't know how many young it has, the waters it patrols, how long it lives, what its general food is, or much else. It's a bit of a disgrace that we can't learn more about it.

* * * * *

How common are White Shark attacks? Not very. Along America's New England coast, the last fatality was in 1936. In Hawaiian waters, the White is extremely rare; though there have been a handful of recorded incidents, the last known death from the White was in 1969. In Hawaii, scientists aren't even certain whether the shark lives there or just visits from time to time to dine on the monk seal during pupping season.

Australia, for all its shark activity, has recorded only a hundred deaths from Whites in 150 years. Throughout the *world*, deaths from these creatures average a mere ten per year.

Of course, we can only tally what we can record. How many other deaths do we not know about? How many missing swimmers have become lunch? How many wrecked sailors have become dinner?

But look at it this way: Let's say that more than ten people are killed by White Sharks each year. Let's say five times that number, as many as fifty. In the United States alone here's what we find:

- Nearly 50,000 people a year killed in auto accidents
- 600 people killed annually by running their cars into trains
- 3,000 each year choked to death on their own food

- Almost 200 dying per year by home electrocution
- About 100 killed by lightning
- Around 400 dying annually in their own swimming pools
- More than 1,000 dying yearly in recreational boating accidents
- Another 1,000 killed each year by falling objects

I'm certainly not suggesting that one should skinny-dip off California's "Red Triangle," but given the oceans or the overpass, you're safer in the water.

The aspect of danger, when it comes to White Sharks, is a valuable commodity to many. More research grants are awarded to scientists on the basis of protecting the populace than on shark propulsion methods. Offer the television networks a script like "Jaws" and one about shark migratory patterns, and guess which one will bring the bigger bucks.

For many years Australia and South Africa have been known as the White Shark capitals of the world, but that dubious honor has swung to North America, principally to a ninety-mile coastline off Northern California from Monterey Bay to Point Reyes. From 1950-1955 sharks attacked only three people in these waters; a dozen have been hit in just the past four years.

In 1972 the Federal government passed the much needed Marine Mammal Protection Act, to prevent the extinction of such animals as seals and sea otters, previously slaughtered mercilessly by pelt hunters. The result of this change, naturally, was increased numbers of what White Sharks feed on. More shark food means more sharks; more sharks means more shark encounters.

Generally, however, the death rate from White Shark attacks along this coastal area is about one every eight years, though recent evidence suggests this number may be on an alarming incline. Along the entire California coast, there have averaged two White Shark attacks per year since 1950. Government records reflect about sixty-five cases off California since 1926, five resulting in death.

In December, 1986, a young spearfisherman was hit by a 12′–15′ Great White just inside California's Monterey Bay; though quite seriously injured, Frank Gallo survived to dive again in those same waters just three months later. A very courageous and realistic man.

When it comes to methods of eating, sharks, like people, have their individual behavior. For years researchers believed that when Whites bit humans, they would then let them go as perhaps unpalatable. Current thinking, though, is that the animal withdraws after that single bite to wait for the victim to bleed to death or become sufficiently immobile as to no longer be a threat before going back to feed. It's thought that this behavior is simply a wise method the shark employs to avoid injury from a struggling sea lion or other pinniped prey.

Film studies have shown five basic approach-behaviors when White Sharks go after bait. In the occasional Surface Charge, we see the animal churn up the water while swimming partially above the surface in a surprisingly rapid rush toward its target.

The Side Roll happens now and then with submerged baits, when the shark tips fifty or sixty degrees on its side, mouth open, to engulf the chunk of food without having to raise its head or fully open its large mouth.

An even less-seen eating posture is called the Inverted Approach. Here, Whites go toward the bait straight on, and then roll over on their backs to almost lazily gulp it. (It's been claimed that this behavior is reserved for those animals who had been feeding for some time in the same area and were in comparatively low states of excitement.)

The Underwater Approach is considered the most common method White Sharks use for bait that is floating on the surface. In this case, the animal swims a foot or so under water, after numerous cautious circles at the periphery, then comes directly toward the food until about three feet away—at which point it raises its head sharply, often rolls its eyes back, juts its protruding upper jaw beyond its lips, and bites or even swallows the twenty-pound morsel whole. At these times both divers and onboard observers can often hear a "barking" sound as air and water rush into the shark's mouth and are then forcibly ejected.

And finally, there is the Normal Underwater Pass where the shark swims below the surface, again after long, careful scrutiny of its object, speeds toward it, and in one second has arched its head back and grabbed the bait.

All these, naturally, depend on the shark's size, perhaps its age, the relation of the bait to the surface, the shark's excitation state, the size and type of bait and so forth.

CHAPTER FIVE

Staying Out Of Trouble

THERE ARE AS MANY PIECES OF advice as there are experts and survivors. Some will tell you to wear only bright clothes while in the water, so you don't look like a porpoise from below; others say that Whites are attracted to bright reds or oranges, so *only* wear black. Maybe both are correct, or we should only go into the water attired in green and yellow paisley. No one knows for sure what colors appeal to sharks.

Nonetheless, there are some basics on which all shark authorities agree. Keeping them in mind won't guarantee safety, but it'll help.

Don't go in the ocean alone.

There are amazingly few cases of a shark attacking two people, or even of Whites going after a person who is coming to a victim's aid.

Stay away from speared or wounded fish.

If you're a spear fisherman, get your catch onto shore or in your boat as soon as possible. Having them dangling from a stringer attached to your body is pure stupidity if you're in waters known to contain sharks. Numerous are the accounts of people being bit by accident when the animal was actually aiming for a speared fish.

Keep blood out of the water.

Even though some experts argue about the degree to which Great Whites or other sharks are attracted to blood, you're better off playing it safe if you have a severe wound.

Have a weapon.

If you know you'll be doing submerged diving in waters where sharks live, take along a sturdy stick, or plan to use your speargun. These implements won't wound a shark, but will surely help you keep one at bay until someone comes.

Shark observers regularly use balloons to keep the bait floating near the surface.

Be alert.

Great Whites seem to just materialize, so whenever you're in temperate oceans, keep on the lookout at all times, and don't let up your vigilance for an instant. That's not to say swim in constant fear, but simply be aware of what's around you, and where you are in relation to such obstacles of escape as a sea wall or coral reef.

Stay cool.

Should you see a White or other shark, you must maintain your wits. A slow, deliberate exit makes a lot more sense than flailing madly as you try outswimming it. You won't. Keep your eye on the animal at all times, even if this means you have to scuttle backward.

Remain submerged.

Assuming you are a diver on scuba, that is. Check your available air, then stay under water—watching the shark as you patiently work your way to safety. You'll be able to observe the shark much better when submerged.

If worse comes to worst . . .

You're cornered by a Great White and it clearly has you on its mind. All of the above tips have been considered or tried, and it's coming right at you. *Act madly frantic:* This may sound silly, but some have survived potential attacks by doing just this; wave wildly with your arms and legs, perhaps showing that you're not a smooth-shaped fish or seal. *Yell:* Yep, this is possible under water, and under these circumstances may not even be preventable; and yes, a hearty scream has been known to deter aggressive sharks. *Give it a punch*: If the White is this close, there's not much more you can do, anyway, so a sock on the snout is worth a try, and many a survivor is alive today because of this very basic technique. *Go for the eyes:* Granted, this is a last resort because by this time you and the shark are on a first-name basis; nonetheless, the eyes are the White's most vulnerable area, which is why it often rolls them back when it attacks.

When all else fails, pray. Who knows?

Right, a huge Great White passes by, fortunately ignoring the air hose connecting a tied-in scuba tank to the author's air-giving regulator.

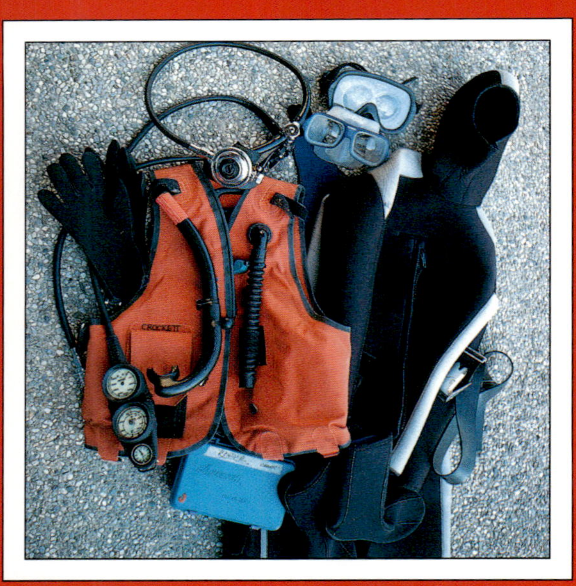
CROCKETT

CHAPTER SIX

Getting There Is Half The Fun

TRAVELLING THOUSANDS OF miles to Australia isn't something one is likely to do on the spur of the moment. And one doesn't spontaneously stand in line to board a shark boat.

At this writing only one scuba travel operation, San Francisco's See and Sea Travel, continues to organize photographic safaris to Great White territory, and this just once a year. It seems that while there are surely hundreds of thousands, perhaps millions, of people interested in White Sharks, barely a half-dozen amateurs per year actually make such trips. The reasons are numerous: cost, time and that one must be a certified scuba diver of some experience. The most common reason so few make the trek, however, is emotional—when it comes right down to it, not everyone is cut out for the hours of underwater solitude in wait, nor for the intensity when a 15′, 2500 pound Great White comes right after you, even within the sanctuary of the cage. More than once a tourist diver has sat out the rest of the trip onboard after that first shark encounter. And then there is the matter of the spouse: Not many husbands or wives are willing to wait home anxiously while their mate is perhaps half-way around the world baiting and encountering Great White Sharks. Of the hundreds of people who write See and Sea for literature on the trip, coming up with six or seven takers is no easy matter for organizer Carl Roessler.

On such trips, you first fly to Sydney and after spending a couple of days to get over the time change and the exhaustion of travel, you make two shorter flights, finally settling in the harbor town of Port Lincoln in the state of South Australia. You've lugged your personal suitcase, a substantial bag of dive gear, and every bit of photo equipment you could round up. Some have even hauled submersible video cameras and TV monitors (on one trip I made, a diver so prepared made one tiny mistake—he forgot to utilize a transformer for the boat's different electrical system; plugging in the monitor for an evening's exciting viewing, he blew up the system).

In Port Lincoln you customarily spend a night at a local motel so you're

MARINER
64

ready for the early car ride to the boat to load, establish bunks, and then depart.

While the entire excursion requires a couple of weeks' time, half of that is taken up with the long flight to Australia, two days to visit Sidney, waiting for other plane connections, the ensuing flights, the motel stay, and so forth. And then, you're on board.

What to bring.

Cool clothes for the sunny days, of course, but don't forget warm pants, sweaters, and jackets—the nights can get quite cold, the wind can kick up, and that 3 a.m. watch can be a bit brisk. Sun lotion, books, a journal, favored snacks and other "musts" for such trips, naturally.

Dive gear calls for some specific attention. Leave your 1/8" warm water wet suit home; you'll need a toasty 1/4" suit with a hood and booties, because you'll be in low-50° water for hours at a time. If you plan to take photos, and you surely should, you'll want to bring light gloves, because the usual cold-water ones won't give you the flexibility you need to operate a camera underwater.

Inflatable buoyancy compensators aren't necessary on a trip like this because you'll be in the cage just a few feet below the surface; no swimming, so you won't need fins, either. (Some boat trips will make an extra non-shark dive on the way back, however, so check out this possibility before deciding against fins and buoyancy compensators.)

A snorkel isn't usually required since you are so close to the surface, but one can always come in handy, so bring it along anyway. You'll need a weightbelt (weights will be furnished on trips of this type), since you'll be carrying more weight than you might expect—being so near the surface, you'll be more buoyant than on regular dives, and when the water acts up and the cage bobs around frantically, you'll benefit from the stability seemingly excess weight offers as you're trying to take pictures. Along this line, you might consult your doctor in advance for seasickness preventatives; I've been on many dive boats over the years, and I've only been sick twice—in South Australia, on the way to the Great Whites.

Of course you'll need your regulator and mask; an extra mask would be a good idea, too, since you surely don't want your trip ruined if one gets lost or if a strap breaks.

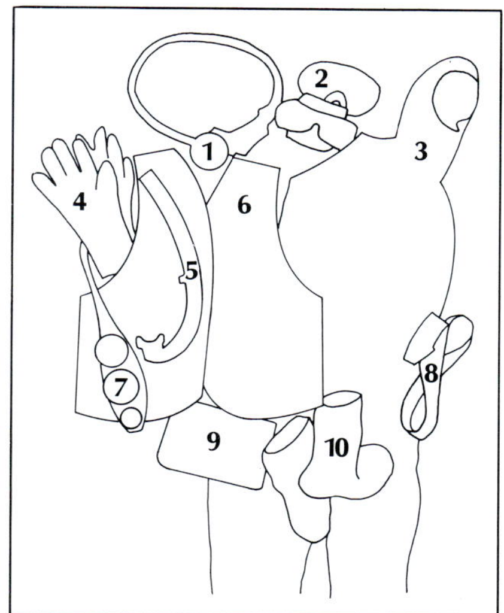

1, regulator; 2, masks; 3, hooded 1/4″ wetsuit (or a dry suit); 4, gloves; 5, snorkel; 6, buoyancy compensator (only needed for additional non-cage dives, otherwise a backpack will do); 7, air pressure gauge (plus depth gauge for use on extra dives); 8, weight belt; 9, repair kit; 10, booties. Fins are only used for added dives. Also, a general gear bag to keep all this together on board.

As on any dive trip, bring personal first-aid supplies, repair tools, and anything else you think you might need. Remember, you're fifty miles out to sea, and your companions won't take kindly to your request to head back to port because you forgot sunscreen.

ROBERTA POOLE-CROCKETT

CHAPTER SEVEN

Taking Pictures Is The Other Half

THERE ARE TWO PHOTOgraphic aspects to a great White Shark trip: topside and underwater. Both are equally as exciting and rewarding. And each presents its own challenges.

Surface photography is dramatically varied. On occasion the boat will seek shelter from rough seas by anchoring near small, uninhabited islands—perfect sunset stuff, for instance, as the Australian sky over an abandoned shack turns golden.

For example, during waiting hours fifty miles out, you may have the opportunity to prowl among sea lions on the tiny islands that have been their homes for hundreds of years. Closeups of pups are a "must," as are portraits of majestic bulls that seem to survey their domain and harems.

Onboard, too, photo opportunities are everywhere for those with eyes to see them. The boat itself may be an uninspiring converted shrimper, but don't get discouraged. There are the divers and crew, naturally, but you can also capture the boat from the dinghy if you want. Look for the unusual, those detail shots that will add to your mandatory slide show when you return home: the chum buckets (even that nasty-looking ladle), the coils of ropes and hoses, the rigging, the cages before they've been set over the side, your meals in the galley, even your below-deck cramped but memorable bunk.

There's more, too. Catch the lowering of the cages in between lending a hand to help settle them into the water. A shot of the fish-oil slick trailing for miles from the rear will show friends how sharks are attracted in the first place. And don't forget the bait—it may look ghastly, but it's an integral part of your slide show; after all, without bait you won't have much of a story to tell. Be ready for anything. On my second excursion we saw a double-rainbow, my one and only.

And watch for fins.

The classic surface Great White shot, a fin cutting the water. Sure it's a cliché; sure it's hackneyed; but sure it's breathtaking. Talk about an opener

1, three Nikonos cameras with 15mm, 28mm, and 35mm lenses; 2, properly identified hard case; 3, cage bag, Polaroid filter, small zoon and wide angle surface lenses; 4, repair and parts kit; 5, film in lead-lined bag for protection from airport X-rays. Plus, your land camera.

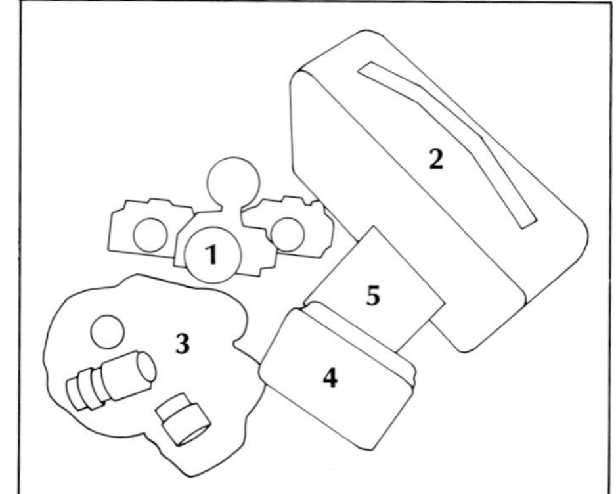

sima
FOR AIR TRAVELERS
LEAD LAMINATED POUCH

for your slide viewing. But be sure your lens is equipped with a polarizing filter because the water's glare can wipe out what seems so clear through your sunglasses.

Surface shark photos can be as dramatic as the underwater ones. Nearly. Whites may come right to the boat, taking a sampling nip here and there from the metal rear platform. And when a shark takes a bait at the surface, you'll have all you can do to keep your wits about you as the animal thrashes side to side, even coming a foot or more out of the water. Pre-focus your lens to where you expect action, because when it's shark time you won't want to be checking your lens setting. If you have a motor drive, bring it; if you don't have one, get one—it may cost you a few bucks, but you won't be returning to Australia very soon, and you'll kick yourself blue when you return home and realize what potentially extraordinary shots you missed. The action, when the sharks come in for bait, will be lightning-fast, the foam will be flying and you'll get splashed when the massive tail slings around. Then, just when it seems like the shark has left, there it'll be, right in front of you, its mouth wide open, the teeth gleaming—will you be ready?

Lenses? For topside work a wide-angle is a "must" for those expansive seascapes. A small zoom is another necessity, allowing you to quickly frame an oncoming White, and then be set when it powers right up next to the boat to grab a bait. Additional lenses are always handy, but these two are required.

Underwater photography has many similarities to topside work, but, as you can envision, there are a few crucial differences. For one thing, changing rolls of film underwater isn't recommended—unless you're in a submarine. The same goes for switching lenses. Now, you've come too far, and invested too much money, to find that you shot exposure #36 just as two more Great Whites appear in front of your cage. Since you can't pop in another roll of Kodachrome, the only practical solution is to carry two or more submersible cameras into the cage with you: Keep one in your hand, another strapped around your neck, then possibly a third one in an old cloth bag tied to the side of the cage. This way, when one roll is finished, you just switch to one of the other cameras.

Some photographers mount their land cameras in watersafe plastic housings, rather than utilize self-contained underwater cameras such as the

popular Nikonos series that most diver/photographers use. On the one hand, the quality from an excellent 35mm single-lens reflex may be marginally better, but you'll be dealing with a rather cumbersome box in the cramped quarters of, say, a 3'x 5' cage shared by three of you simultaneously trying to keep your balance and control the adrenalin. And then imagine bringing three housed cameras with you. Unless you have clear reasons for a housed camera, stick to the Nikonos.

Normally, Nikonos cameras come equipped with a standard 35mm lens. It's a decent piece, and one of the few lenses that works as well underwater as it does above, but for shots of immense Great White Sharks swimming around and up to your cage, a wide-angle is the perfect ticket. Here I recommend my favorite lens, the 15mm; it's not the least expensive you've ever priced, but comparative shopping can yield reasonable savings. With the 15mm, you can focus on a shark just a couple of feet away and still get the whole animal in the frame. This way, too, there is less water between you and the shark when you trip the shutter, and less water equals a clearer photo.

With two or three cameras on hand, having an equal number of 15s might strain the budget a bit. Here's where the less expensive 28mm moderate wide-angle is the perfect compromise. It won't give you all that the 15 will, but it's a good alternative. Then, if you bring a third camera into the cage, your stock 35mm will make an adequate backup until you're back on the boat to reload the wide-angle units.

For film, I suggest Kodachrome or Fuji, though you should certainly use any other fine slide film if you have a preference. And I suggest a lot of it. With slide film rather than print film, your color saturation will be better, plus it won't be quite so costly when you eliminate the outtakes. In general, you should bring cannisters of ISO 64-rated film, since most of your photographs will be taken 5' or less from the surface, where you'll have plenty of light. The new Kodachrome ISO 200 will be perfect for late afternoon shots. These films will do the job topside as well.

I took the underwater pictures in this book with Nikonos IV-A cameras equipped with a 15mm wide-angle Nikkor underwater lens, a 28mm Nikkor and a 35mm Nikkor. The surface photos were shot with a Nikon FA fitted with a Nikkor 35-105 zoom and a 28mm wide-angle. The film was Kodachrome 64 and Ektachrome 200.

I wish I could list all the *f*-stops and shutter speeds, but I can't. You won't be able to either. When the action happens, that's not the time for notes. Probably most of the work was taken at *f*-5.6 and 1/90th.

All the careful pre-planning in the world won't help in shark cage photography. You're in the water for hours at a time, and the light is changing continuously. You may be set for high-noon brightness, and a cloud will blow over, or someone onboard will dump a few cups of chum on your cage. You may adjust everything for dim, murky water, just to have the shark flare its bright white underside right in front of your lens. Or, you'll have the distance set for infinity only to be instantly surprised as a White Shark mouths your cage a few inches away. I could go on.

What to do? What any other intelligent photographer does—bring more film than clothes. Shoot everything in sight, with every setting on the camera. And then hope like crazy that a handful comes out decently. Film is the cheapest part of a venture like this, so don't scrimp.

Afterword

PEOPLE HAVE KILLED COUNTLESS more sharks than sharks have killed people. For one thing, we can go into their territory; they can't come into ours. We've used nets to snare or strangle them, powerheads to blow them up, spears to puncture them, hooks to snag them. For so long we've thought White Sharks were put on this earth simply to terrify us. So intense was the national hatred that, in 1916, President Woodrow Wilson postponed a Cabinet meeting about World War I to discuss how to rid the East Coast of sharks!

But we're beginning to act with intelligence rather than fear; knowledge rather than ignorance. We have, however, a tremendously long way to go. Today, not only scientists and filmmakers can see what the White Shark is like in its own surroundings, so can people like you and me if we're certified scuba divers. It seems impossible to me that anyone who has been in the water observing the Great White could come away with anything but respect and admiration for this magnificent animal, so perfectly at one with its environment.

I've sat onboard shark boats, jotting down the adjectives divers use when casually describing to one another what they've experienced. From my notes: *majestic, marvelous, beautiful, graceful, cautious, peaceful, legendary, powerful, shy, magical*. I have no record of these divers using such words as treacherous, vicious, man-eating, cold-hearted, violent.

The oceans are filled with swimmers as well as sharks. And with only incredibly rare exceptions, both parties get along just fine. Wouldn't it be an absolute crime if we were to set about wiping out a species of animal that has existed for 400 million years?

Thanks

. . . to Carl Roessler who has created the system that first allowed me to experience the White Shark. His photographic artistry along with his love of the sea and its creatures have inspired many thousands of divers and environmentalists all over the world.

. . . to Rodney Fox who showed us all that not only can we rise above devastating injury, but we can also rise above killing, as he did by dedicating his life to showing the world what a wondrous creature the White Shark is.

. . . to John McCosker, Director of San Francisco's Steinhart Aquarium, whose years of research have been absorbed by so many others as part of the accepted knowledge of this most captivating of the sea's creatures.

. . . to my wife Bobi, who willingly postponed our wedding so I could take another trip in the cages.

. . . and to Alan, Chris, Paul, Jake, Cheryl, Leslie, Roger, Oma and Opa, Cheńoa, Laurenne, Cordell, Kessel, Devon and especially Bonnie.

Some Personal Thoughts

SHARKS ARE HARD TO FIND. You can scuba dive for years without seeing one. But when a diver does come across a shark, any shark, it's cause for topside jubilation. Even a tiny foot-long Horn Shark will captivate a diver.

So, when I saw my first—a Black Tip, I think—I was mesmerized. It was only 5′ long, cruising around in shallow Tahitian water, just minding its own business about 20′ away. I stared, captivated that I'd finally seen a shark, and it was a beauty. So sleek, so graceful. I tried getting closer, but it would have none of that, and staying just slightly faster than I, it slid away and was eventually lost from view in the rather turbid water that day in 1982.

Like so many millions of others, I'd often found myself gravitating to the shark tanks when I visited aquariums. No idea why; just something mystical or maybe magical about them. So, when I got a flyer in the mail, offering, among other trips, a chance to see the Great White eye-to-eye, it was an opportunity I couldn't pass up.

There were only five of us that time, and I had a breathtaking trip, coming back with a thousand or more slides (a dozen were even worth showing around). I talked about the adventure with my fiancée and a few friends, but kept the real importance of it to myself—it was just too difficult to describe the impact and meaning it had for me.

Two years later. Fiancée was about to become wife. Our date was set. Then I got another mailer. Such a dilemma. I knew how much I wanted to go back to take all those photos I'd missed. But the departure date coincided exactly with the wedding date. I tossed the leaflet on the table, telling Bobi that—being a diver herself—she might like to see the terrific Carl Roessler photographs it contained.

"Hey, there's another Great White trip," she announced. "You going?"

"It leaves the day we're getting married," I said, a slight whine to my voice, no doubt.

"We can always change the wedding plans."

Not the typical fiancée response, certainly, but the typical diver response.

Trip number two, even for an "experienced" hand like myself, was just as special as the first. And the photos came out better.

A book? Not a bad idea. I hired my daughter Laurenne, a recent UCLA graduate, as my research assistant, and began sorting through the mountain of slides, pages of trip journals, and complex personal feelings about this complex fascinating creature.

Will I go back a third time? Well, I'm already up to my waist in pictures, I've lived an experience few people will ever know, I've been . . .

Sources

Books

Animal Facts and Feats. Gerald L. Wood/Guinness Superlatives, Ltd., Doubleday & Co. Inc., Garden City, N.Y. 1972.
Book of Sharks, The. Richard Ellis. Grosset & Dunlap, N.Y. 1976.
Dictionary of Fishes. 11th Ed. Allyn Rube. Great Outdoors Publications, Co., 1967.
Fresh and Salt Water Fishes of the World, The. Edward C. Migdalski and George S. Fichter. Alfred A. Knopf, N.Y. 1976.
Grzimek's Animal Life Encyclopedia, Vol. 4. Litton World Trade Corporation, 1973.
Life of Sharks, The. Paul Budker. Columbia University Press, N.Y. 1971.
Myth and Maneater. D.K. Webster. W.W. Norton & Co., Inc. N.Y. 1962.
Oceanus Vol. 24, No. 4. Winter 1981/1982.
Sensory Biology of Sharks, Skates, and Rays. Office of Naval Research, Dept. of the Navy. Arlington, VA. 1978.
Shark Attack. H. David Baldridge. Droke House, Anderson, South Carolina. 1974.
Sharks, The. Robert F. Burgess. Doubleday & Co., Inc. Garden City, N.Y. 1970.
Sharks and Rays. Spencer Wilkie Tinker & Charles J. Deluca. Charles E. Tuttle Co., Inc., VT & Tokyo, Japan. 1973.
Sharks: Attacks and Adventures with Rodney Fox, Olaf Ruhen. White Pointer Enterprises. Melbourne, Australia. 1975.
Sharks: Killers of the Deep. Michael Bright. Multimedia Publications, Gallery Books. New York, NY. 1984.
Sharks: Lord of the Sea. Sandra Romashko. Windward Publishing, Miami, Florida. 1979.
Southern California Academy of Sciences, Memoirs, Vol. 9, 1985.
"Areal Distribution and Autoecology of the White Shark, Carcharodon carcharias, off the West Coast of North America, The" A. Peter Klimey.
"Dynamics of White Shark/Pinniped Interactions in the Gulf of the Farallones," David G. Ainley, R. Philip Henderson, Harriet R. Huber, Robert J. Bockelheide, Sarah G. Allen, and Teresa L. McElroy.
"Feeding Ethology of the White Shark, Carcharodon carcharias," Timothy C. Tricas.

"Hematology and Cardiac Morphology in the Great White Shark, Carcharodon carcharias," Scott H. Emery.

"Preliminary Studies on the Age and Growth of the White Shark, Carcharodon carcharias, Using Vertebral Bands," Gregor M. Cailliet, Lisa J. Natanson, Bruce A. Welden, David A. Ebert.

"Shark Attacks off the California and Oregon Coasts: An Update, 1980-1984," Robert N. Lea and Daniel J. Miller.

"Temperature, Heat Production and Heat Exchange in Lamnid Sharks," Francis G. Carey, John G. Casey, Harold L. Pratt, David Urquhart, and John E. McCosker.

"Visual System of the White Shark, Carcharodon carcharias, with Emphasis on Retinal Structure," Samuel H. Gruber, Joel L. Cohen.

"White Sharks in Hawaii: Historical and Contemporary Records," Leighton Taylor.

Periodicals, Papers, and Pamphlets

"Accident Facts," 1984 edition. National Safety Council.

"Dangers of the Red Triangle," *Time Magazine*, November 19, 1984.

"Expert Calls Great Whites Slow, Clumsy," David Perlman, *San Francisco Chronicle*, February 18, 1985.

"Filming the Great White Sharks," Valerie Taylor, *Oceans Magazine*, Number 6, 1983.

"The Great White," Tom Stienstra, *San Francisco Examiner*, March 16, 1986.

"The Great White Hope," Tom Bates. *California Magazine*, March, 1984.

"The Great White Shark," Erin Hopkins. Unpublished paper. Honolulu, Hawaii.

"In Praise of Sharks," E.O. Wilson, *Discover Magazine*, July, 1985.

"Life After Jaws," Hillary Hauser, *Oceans Magazine*, November, 1983.

"On The Track of the Real Shark," Shannon Brownlee, *Discover Magazine*, July, 1985.

"Sharks Are Cuddly? Well, No, But They Aren't So Bad, Either," James Sterba, *Wall Street Journal*, July 22, 1983.

"Sharks, Parts I and II," Chaco Mohler. *Windsurf Magazine*, March and April, 1986.

Index